Claire
(the author)

Kate
(the illustrator)

First published in 2007

10 9 8 7 6 5 4 3 2 1

1TR/0407/TECH/SCHOY/157MA/C

Copyright © Kingfisher Publications Plc 2007
Text and concept © Claire Llewellyn 2007

Consultant: Dr. Phil Manning, lecturer in paleontology,
University of Manchester, U.K.
Managing editor: Carron Brown
Coordinating editor: Caitlin Doyle
Designer: Amy McSimpson
DTP manager: Nicky Studdart
Senior production controller: Jessamy Oldfield
Cover designer: Jo Connor

LIBRARY OF CONGRESS CATALOGING-IN-PUBLICATION DATA
Llewellyn, Claire.
    Ask Dr. K. Fisher about animals / Claire Llewellyn.—1st ed.
      p. cm.
    Includes index.
    ISBN: 978-0-7534-6106-8
    1. Dinosaurs—Miscellanea—Juvenile literature. I. Title.
QE861.5.L545 2007
567.9—dc22   2006034406

Printed in China

*For my nephew, Arthur, and for my
friend Sam. With fondest love—K. S.*

KINGFISHER

a Houghton Mifflin Company

imprint 222 Berkeley Street

Boston, Massachusetts 2116

www.houghtonmifflinbooks.com

Ask Dr. K. Fisher about . . .

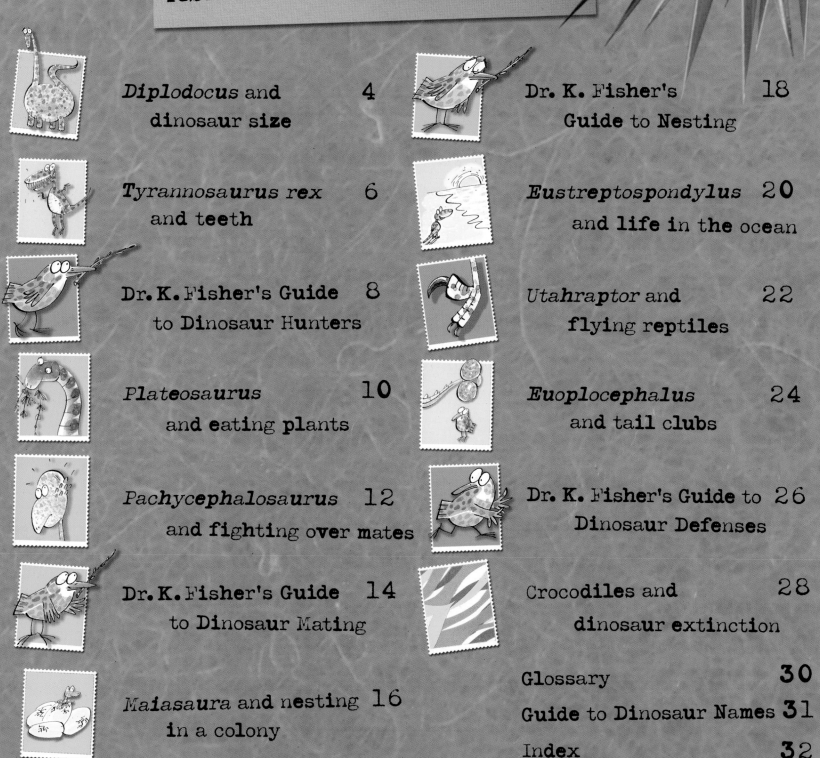

Here's a huge Diplodocus

A weighty problem

Dear Dr. K. Fisher,

I'm a young female Diplodocus that likes to watch her weight, but recently it's skyrocketed! I've put on a ton this year, and the smaller, slimmer dinosaurs are laughing at me. Yes, I do eat a lot, but it's all greens, and I never touch fast food! What am I doing wrong?

Monumental, in the meadow

Diplodocus

Ornitholestes

4

Dr. K. Fisher
Any problem solved!
1 Diving-in-the-Water
Birdsville 54321

Dear **Monumental,**

Don't worry—you are perfectly normal. A *Diplodocus* has a lot of growing to do. When you hatch from your egg, you measure around three feet long, but as an adult you weigh 40 tons and are almost 120 feet long! You belong to a group of dinosaurs called sauropods— and your size is the key to your success. You're too big to be troubled by predators, and, towering above the trees like you do, you can feed on the leaves that other dinosaurs cannot reach.

Happy eating!

Dr. K. Fisher

Teething troubles

Tyrannosaurus rex

Dear Dr. K. Fisher,
I'm a Tyrannosaurus rex, and I have a dental issue. I'm still young, but my teeth are falling out. I'm supposed to be the scariest hunter on Earth, but I can't frighten anyone with my bare gums. What's going on?

Toothless Killer, up the creek

Edmontosaurus

Triceratops

6

Dr. K. Fisher
Any problem solved!
1 Diving-in-the-Water
Birdsville 54321

Dear **Toothless Killer,**

I can understand your concern. Your teeth are important weapons. Sharp, saw-edged, and up to seven inches long, they are great for biting and shaking your prey and piercing through their leathery hides. That's why a few of your teeth are falling out! But, don't worry, all carnivorous dinosaurs grow new teeth to replace the ones that they lose. Rest assured that you will never lose your toothy grin and your useful bite!

Respectfully yours,

Dr. K. Fisher

Turn the page for **more about dinosaur hunters ...**

7

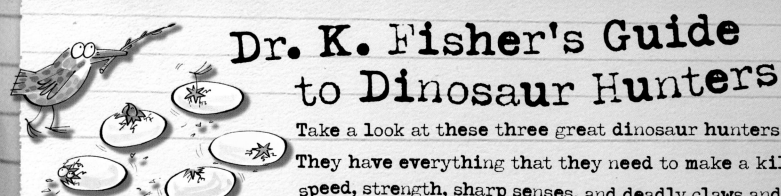

Dr. K. Fisher's Guide to Dinosaur Hunters

Take a look at **these three** great **dinosaur hunters.**

They **have everything** that **they need** to **make a kill**—
speed, strength, sharp senses, and **deadly claws and teeth.**

Compsognathus

Height: 20 inches
Weight: 6.6 pounds
Preys on: Insects, lizards, and mammals
Deadly features:
- Sharp eyes
- Long, narrow jaws with small, sharp teeth
- Three-fingered clawed hands to grip prey
- Long legs for fast running
- Clawed feet to pin down prey

Height: 10 feet
Weight: 130 pounds
Preys on: Lizards and small mammals; attacks larger dinosaurs when hunting in a pack
Deadly features:
- Long, strong arms to seize prey
- Grasping hands and large, sharp claws
- Powerful legs for running and jumping
- Huge claw on second toe springs out like a grapple so that the dinosaur can climb up the body of its prey

Deinonychus

8

Height: 40 feet
Weight: 3 tons
Preys on: Medium and large plant-eating dinosaurs such as *Diplodocus*

Deadly features:
- Large, powerful body is fast and agile
- Huge, gaping jaws deliver killer blows
- Long, sharp, saw-edged teeth tear at prey
- Strong arms with hooklike talons grasp prey
- Three strong toes with sharp claws

Allosaurus

Dr. K. Fisher's Top Tips

 DO steal food from smaller dinosaurs. Eating meat that somebody else has caught saves lots of energy. And it's okay to scavenge, too.

 DO stay out of sight when you're shadowing a herd. If the animals see you, they will bunch up together and be harder to attack.

 DON'T choose prey that looks strong and healthy. Always try to pick an animal that is old, sick, or young.

Here's a smelly Plateosaurus

Blowing in the **wind!**

Dear Dr. K. Fisher,
I'm a Plateosaurus, and I have
an embarrassing problem: wind.
It's painful, it's noisy, and (to be honest)
it doesn't smell very nice. I'm afraid
that I'm going to lose my friends in the
herd. Is there anything I can do?

Red-faced,
among the ferns

horsetails

cycads

Plateosaurus

Dr. K. Fisher
Any problem solved!
1 Diving-in-the-Water
Birdsville 54321

Dear Red-faced,

I'm sorry to say that the culprit is your diet. You eat a lot of cycads, horsetails, and araucaria leaves—tough food that's hard for your body to digest. To help with digestion, you plant eaters swallow stones, which sit in the gizzard (stomach number one), grinding your food into softer stuff. When stomach number two has also worked on it, the food passes into your gut, where it ferments and gives off gas. Your friends in the herd share this problem. It's best not to be too sensitive about things that you cannot change.

Best wishes,

Dr. K. Fisher

araucaria tree

11

Butting in

Dear Dr. K. Fisher,

I am a Pachycephalosaurus mom, and I'm worried about my son. He's always been such a nice boy, but recently he's begun head butting the other males in the herd. I'm worried that he's going to hurt himself and get into terrible trouble. What could have brought on this behavior, and is there anything I can do to stop it?

Don't Like Trouble, in the herd

Pachycephalosaurus
(males)

Pachycephalosaurus

(females)

Dr. K. Fisher
Any problem solved!
1 Diving-in-the-Water
Birdsville 54321

Dear **Don't Like Trouble,**

It sounds as if your son has reached the age when he's fighting over females. In your species this is normal behavior. The males run and bash heads with one another just like battering rams. It's their way of finding the strongest male to mate with the females and father their young. Don't worry about him hurting himself: his head is made of almost solid bone, so his brain is well protected.

Kind regards,

Dr. K. Fisher

Turn the page for **more** about dinosaur mating . . .

13

Dr. K. Fisher's Guide
to Dinosaur Mating

How does a **male dinosaur beat the other boys and get a date?**
What is it that makes them so special? Meet some successful
dinosaur males and find out how to win a female's heart.

Tyrannosaurus rex

We *T. rexes* live alone, and females are few
and far between. If I hear one calling for
a mate, I make a quick kill and offer her
the carcass while it's still fresh and juicy.
Tempted?

T. rex . . . loves eating out.

Triceratops

Will you take a look at my horns?
Aren't they the longest and
sharpest? I lock horns with
rivals in the herd until
they cry for mercy.

Triceratops . . . he's a sharp guy.

 # Protoceratops

I have a large neck frill and a big, attractive bump on my nose. The bump comes in handy as a powerful weapon to butt other males out of the way!

Protoceratops . . . has all the frills.

 # Dilophosaurus

I've been blessed with a large, bony crest on the top of my head. When I bob my head up and down, the males see the size of it, and they leave the females to me.

Dilophosaurus . . . is ahead of the rest.

 # Dr. K. Fisher's Top Tips

DO whatever you can to threaten your rivals: bellow loudly, swing your tail, flash your horns, and raise your plates.

DON'T always fight the first male that you see. Take your time and look around. Try to pick on someone smaller than you.

DO back down if you're less threatening than your opponent. Only fight if you know that you can win.

 15

Here's a cooped-up Maiasaura

Give me space!

Dear Dr. K. Fisher,
I'm a female Maiasaura raising my family. I'd hoped to raise my little darlings in a place that I could call my own, but I find myself in a huge nest colony packed with hundreds of other moms. It's so crowded that I'm at the end of my wits. Does it have to be this way?

Melancholy, in the colony

Dr. K. Fisher
1 Diving-in-the-Water
Birdsville 54321

THE COLONY MAIL

DO NOT DISTURB

Maiasaura colony

16

Dr. K. Fisher
Any problem solved!
1 Diving-in-the-Water
Birdsville 54321

Dear **Melancholy,**
Raising your young in a colony is a great way to protect them from danger. A *Maiasaura* knows that there is safety in numbers. While you are finding food for your young, your neighbors will protect them from predators on the prowl. Your time in the colony won't last long. Your hatchlings will soon be strong enough to leave the nest and live on the plains. Next year, you will nest in the colony again. By then it will feel like a home away from home and your neighbors will be good friends.

Good luck!

Dr. K. Fisher

WELCOME

Turn the page for **more about nesting . . .**

Dr. K. Fisher's Guide to Nesting

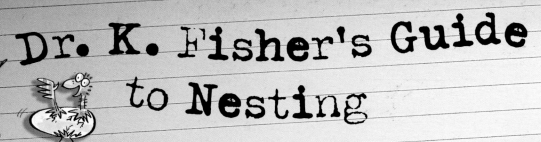

Other dinosaurs nest in colonies too. One of them, an *Oviraptor*, has sent me her family album to explain how she builds her nest and how her babies grow.

Here's yours truly building the nest. I make sure that the rim is nice and high in order to stop my eggs from rolling out.

You wouldn't know it from this photo, but I've just laid 24 beautiful eggs! I'm sitting on the eggs to keep them warm.

Number one hatchling smashes through the shell! Her brothers and sisters are not far behind.

Three more bundles of trouble: my strong little hatchlings leave the nest, ready for their first meals.

Dr. K. Fisher's Top Tips

 DO lay your eggs in neat circles or spirals. Give each egg plenty of space so that your babies have room to hatch.

 DON'T feel like you have to copy the *Oviraptor*. Instead of sitting on your eggs, cover them with a warm layer of plants or soil.

 DON'T worry about the shape of your eggs. Dinosaur eggs can be round, oval, or sausage-shaped.

Here's a Eustreptospondylus *that wants to swim*

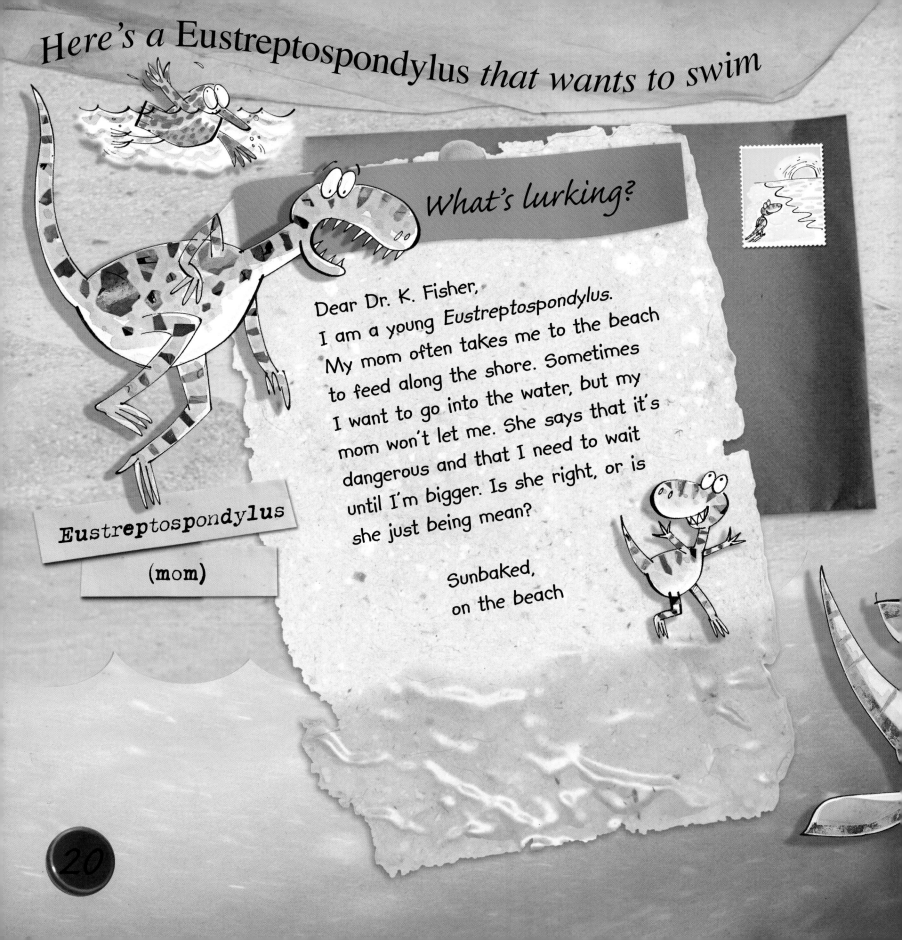

What's lurking?

Dear Dr. K. Fisher,
I am a young Eustreptospondylus.
My mom often takes me to the beach
to feed along the shore. Sometimes
I want to go into the water, but my
mom won't let me. She says that it's
dangerous and that I need to wait
until I'm bigger. Is she right, or is
she just being mean?

Sunbaked,
on the beach

Eustreptospondylus

(mom)

Dr. K. Fisher
Any problem solved!
1 Diving-in-the-Water
Birdsville 54321

Dear **Sunbaked,**

Your mom is right. The oceans are packed with deadly sharks, crocodiles, and giant marine reptiles. There are also ammonites and jellyfish with dangerous tentacles and stingers. You predatory dinosaurs are pretty good swimmers—your bones are light, your legs are strong, and your feet make adequate flippers—but you could get into trouble in the fast currents. It makes sense while you are growing up to stay safe and sound on the shore.

Take care,

Dr. K. Fisher

Liopleurodon

Cryptocleidus

Here's a Utahraptor *that longs to fly*

Want to flap!

Dear Dr. K. Fisher,

I'm a young male Utahraptor, a pretty strong, daredevil type of guy. I'm crazy about pterosaurs. I watch them gather on the cliffs near my home and then jump off and glide through the air. It looks amazing.

How do they do it? Is it hard?

Could I give it a try?

Crazy and Confident,
on a cliff

pterosaurs

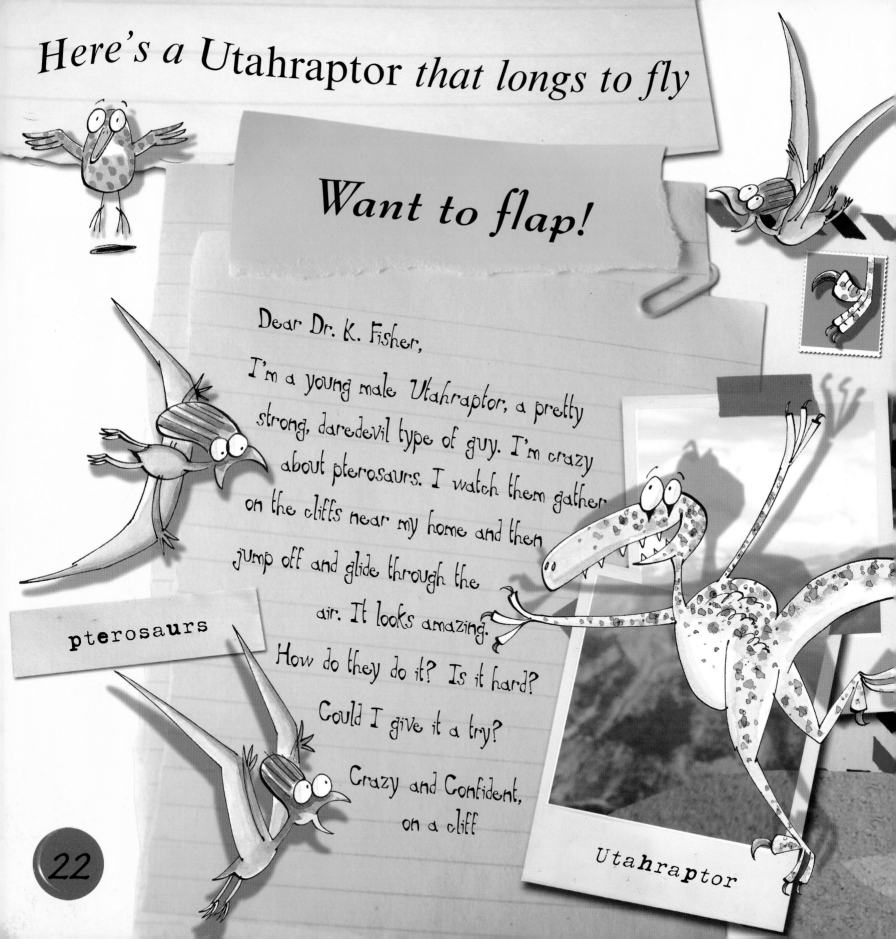

Utahraptor

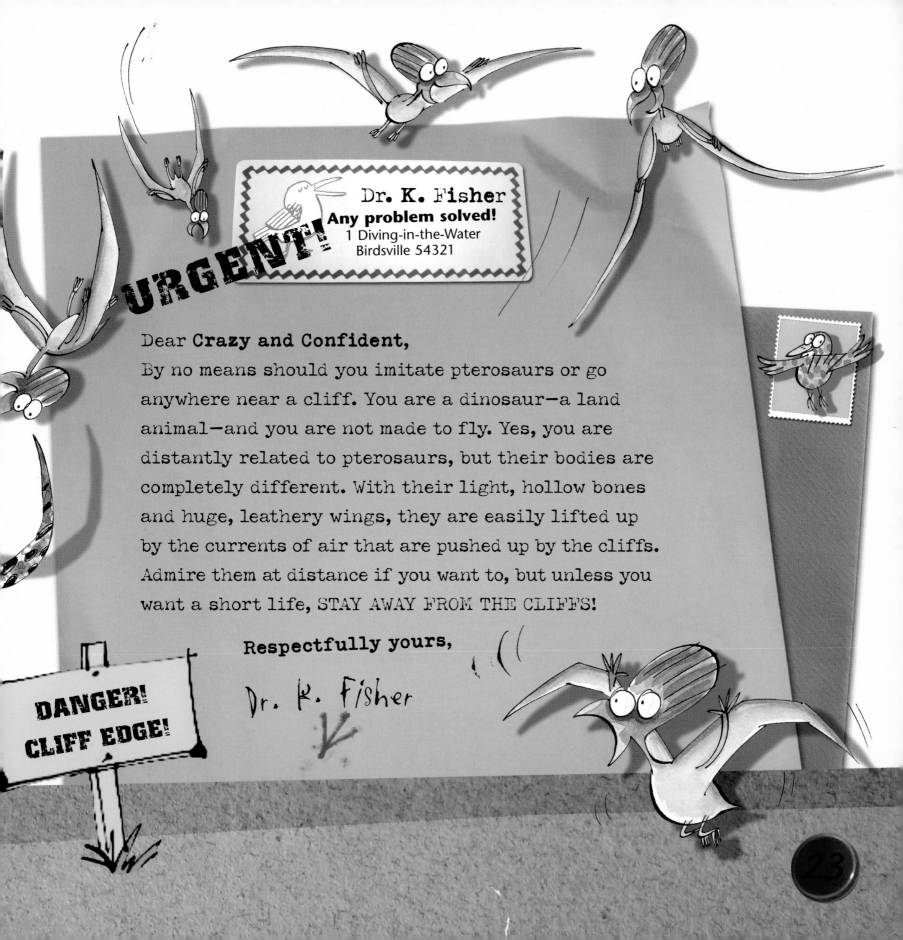

Dr. K. Fisher
Any problem solved!
1 Diving-in-the-Water
Birdsville 54321

Dear **Crazy and Confident,**

By no means should you imitate pterosaurs or go anywhere near a cliff. You are a dinosaur—a land animal—and you are not made to fly. Yes, you are distantly related to pterosaurs, but their bodies are completely different. With their light, hollow bones and huge, leathery wings, they are easily lifted up by the currents of air that are pushed up by the cliffs. Admire them at distance if you want to, but unless you want a short life, STAY AWAY FROM THE CLIFFS!

Respectfully yours,

Dr. K. Fisher

**DANGER!
CLIFF EDGE!**

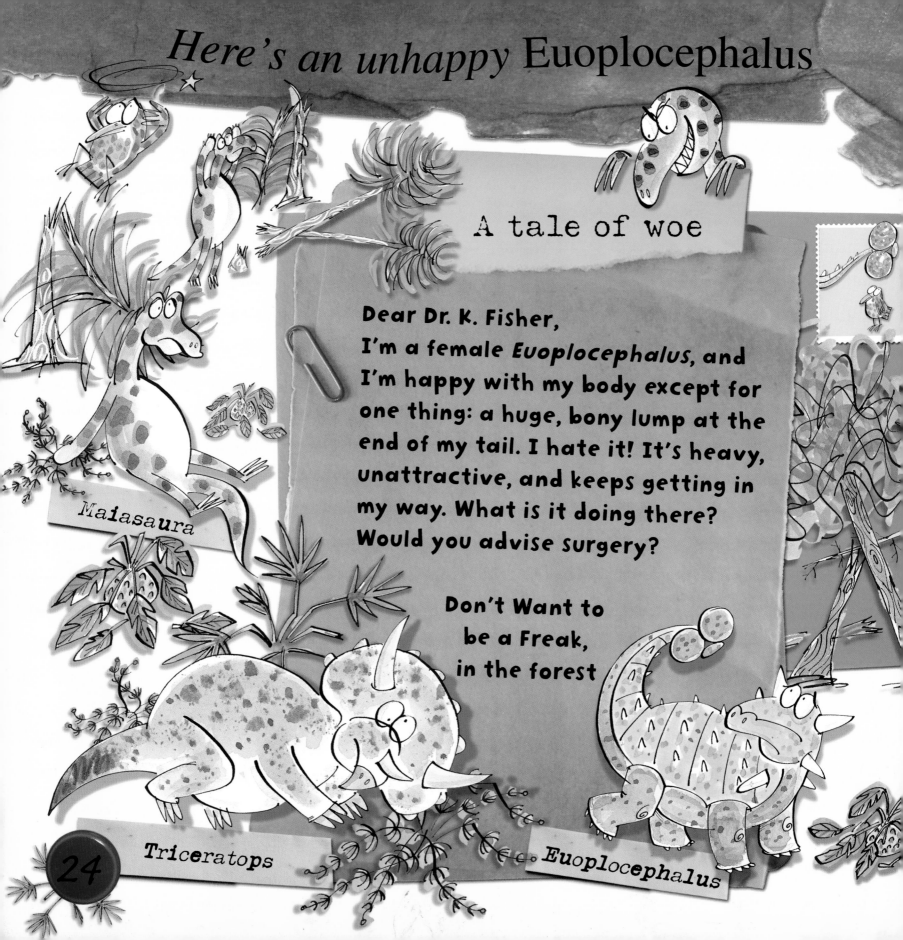

A tale of woe

Dear Dr. K. Fisher,
I'm a female *Euoplocephalus*, and I'm happy with my body except for one thing: a huge, bony lump at the end of my tail. I hate it! It's heavy, unattractive, and keeps getting in my way. What is it doing there? Would you advise surgery?

Don't Want to be a Freak, in the forest

Maiasaura

Triceratops

Euoplocephalus

Dr. K. Fisher
Any problem solved!
1 Diving-in-the-Water
Birdsville 54321

Dear **Don't Want to be a Freak,**

Your bony lump is called a tail club, and it's a great form of defense. When you swing your tail from side to side, you can smash the shins of the largest predators into smithereens. I know that you have other protection—your body is covered in hard, bony plates—but I would still advise against removing your tail club. You must keep all of your defenses intact, especially because you lead a solitary life, without the protection of a herd.

Best wishes,

Dr. K. Fisher

Albertosaurus

(predator)

Turn the page for **more** **25** about **dinosaur defenses . . .**

Dr. K. Fisher's Guide to Dinosaur Defenses

Carnivorous dinosaurs are fast and fierce, so what's the best way for their prey to avoid being eaten? Four defense experts share their experiences.

Ankylosaurus

I'm like an armored tank. I have bony lumps and plates inside my skin. Try to take a bite out of me, and you'll soon get a mouthful of broken teeth!

Stegosaurus

I have sharp spikes on the end of my tail. One good swing sends the heftiest hunter crashing to the ground.

Triceratops

I weigh five tons and have three sharp horns. When I charge at carnivores, I'm unstoppable!

Diplodocus

I'm too big for most predators to catch. If one tries to attack, I whip them with my tail.

Dr. K. Fisher's Top Tips

DO keep your eyes and ears open. **Never** be ashamed to run away at the first sign of danger—it's the best defense there is!

DO crouch down if a predator comes close. This will help protect your soft belly from slashing and biting.

DON'T forget to use your thumb spikes, horns, and any other weapons. You may be a herbivore, but you can still be aggressive!

27

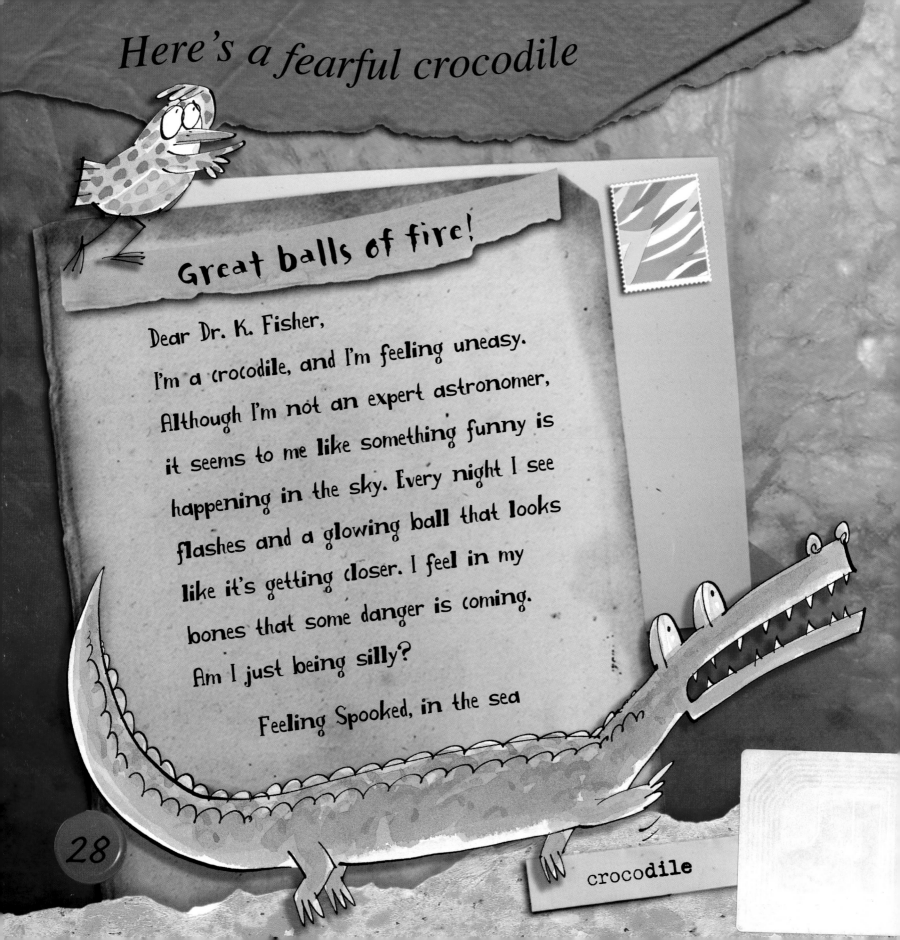

Here's a fearful crocodile

Great balls of fire!

Dear Dr. K. Fisher,

I'm a crocodile, and I'm feeling uneasy. Although I'm not an expert astronomer, it seems to me like something funny is happening in the sky. Every night I see flashes and a glowing ball that looks like it's getting closer. I feel in my bones that some danger is coming. Am I just being silly?

Feeling Spooked, in the sea

28

crocodile

Dr. K. Fisher
Any problem solved!
1 Diving-in-the-Water
Birdsville 54321

Dear **Feeling Spooked,**

Crocodiles, like dinosaurs, have been around for more than 165 million years. You are two of the greatest success stories on Earth. It's true that on our planet species sometimes become extinct. There are a lot of reasons for this: meteors or comets crashing into Earth, massive volcanic eruptions, or huge changes in the climate or sea levels. And yet, even in the biggest extinctions, some species manage to survive into the future. I've got a feeling that you're going to be one of the lucky ones!

All the best,

Dr. K. Fisher

meteor

Pachycephalosaurus

Triceratops

Tyrannosaurus rex

Edmontosaurus

29

Glossary

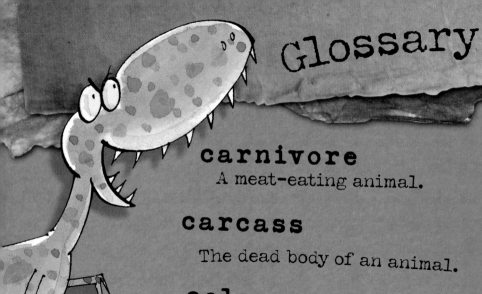

carnivore
A meat-eating animal.

carcass
The dead body of an animal.

colony
A group of animals that live closely together.

comet
A cloud of frozen gas, ice, and dust that travels around the Sun.

current
Air or water that flows in a particular direction.

eruption
When a volcano shoots out gas, ash, and red-hot rocks.

extinct
No longer living on Earth.

ferments
Breaks down, changes, and gives off gas.

gizzard
An extra stomach in some animals that is used to grind tough food.

hide
The skin of an animal.

meteors
Lumps of rocks from space that crash into Earth.

predators
Animals that hunt other animals for food.

prey
Animals that are hunted and eaten by other animals.

pterosaurs
A group of flying reptiles that lived in the age of dinosaurs.

talons
Sharp, hooked claws.

Dr. K.'s Guide to Dinosaur Names

Dinosaurs **have** long Latin names that are **hard** to say. Find out what they **me**an and **how** to pronounce **them** by **using** this handy **gu**ide.

Albertosaurus (al-bert-oh-saw-russ)—means "Alberta lizard"
Allosaurus (al-oh-saw-russ)—means "other lizard"
Ankylosaurus (an-kie-loh-saw-russ)—means "stiff lizard"
Compsognathus (komp-sog-nath-us)—means "elegant jaw"
Deinonychus (die-non-i-kuss)—means "terrible claw"
Dilophosaurus (die-loaf-oh-saw-russ)—means "two-ridge lizard"
Diplodocus (di-plod-oh-kuss)—means "double beam"
Edmontosaurus (ed-mon-toe-saw-russ)—means "Edmonton lizard"
Euoplocephalus (you-oh-plo-kef-ah-lus)—means "well-armored head"
Eustreptospondylus (ewe-strep-toe-spon-die-luss)—means "well-curved vertebra"
Maiasaura (my-ah-sore-ah)—means "good mother lizard"
Ornitholestes (or-nith-oh-les-teez)—means "bird robber"
Oviraptor (oh-vee-rap-tor)—means "egg thief"
Pachycephalosaurus (pack-i-kef-al-oh-saw-russ)—means "thick-headed lizard"
Plateosaurus (plat-ee-oh-saw-russ)—means "first lizard"
Protoceratops (pro-toe-ker-ah-tops)—means "first horned face"
Stegosaurus (steg-oh-saw-russ)—means "roof lizard"
Triceratops (tri-serra-tops)—means "three-horned face"
Tyrannosaurus rex (tie-ran-oh-saw-russ rex)—means "tyrant lizard"
Utahraptor (yoo-tah-rap-tor)—means "Utah plunderer"

Flying reptiles:
pterosaurs (terr-oh-sores)—means "winged lizards"

Marine reptiles:
Liopleurodon (li-ploo-ra-don)—means "smooth-sided tooth"
Cryptocleidus (crip-toe-clide-us)—means "hidden collarbone"

Index